CONNECTING CONVERT

Dr. Gordon S. Jones

Copyright © 2007 Gordon S. Jones
All rights reserved.
ISBN: 149961649X
ISBN-13: 978-1499616491

DEDICATION

To the those, who are driven by the passion and purpose of their Lord and Savior Jesus Christ.

CONTENTS

	Acknowledgments	i
1	Introduction	1

Connecting to the People of Christ

2	Faith	5
3	Repentance	9
4	Confession	13
5	Conversion	17
6	Baptism	20

Connecting to the Purpose of Christ

7	Everyone has to Obey	28
8	Everyone has to Submit	32
9	Everyone has to Participate	34
10	Everyone has to Witness	37

ACKNOWLEDGMENTS

.... to Mary Green, Tiffany Hodge, and Dr. Quincy Quinlan for their touch of excellence on the original manuscript. To A. J. Marshall who experimented with this handbook and have seen the results of his labor.

Thanks to the Alpha Seventh-day Adventist Community for embarking on the journey of disciple-making as opposed to making members.

Finally, to my family for the encouragement, support and sacrifice as we commit to developing discipleship-minded communities.

INTRODUCTION

The gospel commission in Matthew 28:18-20 is undeniably both informative and descriptive. It not only describes who we are, it unequivocally defines what we do. In essence, each Christian is a disciple and a disciple maker and when we neglect doing we cease being. Disciple-making is therefore imperative!

This guide was developed to equip those who endeavor to deliberately fulfill this most important Christian responsibility. It outlines an effective and efficient method in transforming prospective converts into disciples.

Process toward Discipleship

There are essentially three critical connections for successfully discipling converts.

The first connection is a connection to Christ. This is initiated by a desire and choice of a prospective convert to experience a change. This is a personal response to the promptings of the Holy Spirit which leads to a request for baptism. (In this connection the prospect is personally replying to an introduction and invitation to follow Christ, there are no study guides available.)

Second connection is a connection to the people of Christ. This involves the decision and commitment of a prospective convert to personal discipleship. This connection requires an intentional preparation for baptism and demands an understanding of the basic process toward transformation. (The Experience of Salvation study guides are dedicated to assisting with this connection.)

The final connection is a connection to the purpose of Christ. This necessitates the devotion and determination of a disciple to experience spiritual growth. This is the beginning of a lifetime process towards living in a discipleship relationship. (The Essentials of Christian Maturity study guides are dedicated to assisting in this process)

Note to the discipler:

At the end of each chapter there is the Discipler's Tool Kit. This is intended to be a help and guide for those who are purposefully seeking to please God by fulfilling the mandate recorded in Matthew 28: 18 -20 .

*****DISCIPLER'S TOOL KIT*****

Before you begin each first session:

- Review the candidate's decision.
- Schedule your next meeting times/study periods.
- Find out a little about the candidate or candidates you will be studying with.
- Share your personal conversion experience.
- Be sure the prospective disciple has a Bible, notepad, and writing instrument.
- Always begin with prayer.
- Each convert or study group may be comprised of prospectives from varied sources. Below are a few examples:

Connecting Convert

- Visitor packets from your local church.
- A response from a sermon appeal.
- A friend, neighbor, or relative desiring a relationship with Christ.
- Someone you have invited into a discipling relationship

As a discipler you are responsible for:

- Contacting a prospective disciple as soon as possible (best within 24 hours).
- Celebrating the decision for Christ and for change.
- Communicating the steps toward discipleship. (This involves obtaining a commitment from a prospect, to meet consistently.)
- Scheduling a time and a place for your meetings.
- Successfully preparing a prospective disciple for baptism requires:
    o Being polite
    o Being prayerful
    o Being prepared
    o Being punctual

CONNECTING TO THE PEOPLE OF CHRIST

THE EXPERIENCE OF SALVATION

A Preparatory Bible Study Guide for Baptismal Candidates

You will seek me and find me when you seek with all your heart.
Jeremiah 29:13

FAITH

Biblically speaking is advance information given by God concerning God's plans for our lives, this will enable us to experience abundant life now and eternal life hereafter. The purpose of biblical faith is the restoration of the broken relationship between God and humanity. When the relationship between man and God is restored, salvation, which is freedom from sin's penalty, sin's power, and sin's presence, will be realized.

The Source of Faith

Biblical faith does not originate with humans. It is an absolute gift and although revealed in different ways, it is derived from one ultimate source, God Himself.

Romans 12:3 "Because God has given me a special gift. I have something to say to everyone among you. Do not think you are better than you are. You must decide what you really are by the amount of faith God has given you."

It is very important to keep in mind that God is no respecter of persons. He has personally allotted to everyone some amount of faith as He sees fit.

Gordon S. Jones

The Big Idea:
Computers are fitted with stored data that allow them to perform basic functions. These are referred to as system software. However, a user can increase a computer's usability by adding application software. According to Paul in Romans 12: 3, we are all created with a measure of faith (like drivers or system software on the hard drive). In 2 Thessalonians 1:3 Paul states that faith can be increased, (adding application software) and the result is amazing. In 2 Peter 1: 5 – 11, Peter develops the idea that by increasing our faith-base we can add Christian virtues.

God bestows faith in two primary ways

JESUS

Hebrews 12:2 "We do this by keeping our eyes on Jesus, the champion who initiates and perfects our faith. Because of the joy awaiting him, he endured the cross, disregarding its shame. Now he is seated in the place of honor beside God's throne." NTL

We all have been given some measure of faith (biblical information) from God. The problem is how we respond to or apply the information we received. We must be confident that we have all that we need to accomplish God's will and purpose for our lives at the current time.

BIBLE

Romans 10:17 "So faith comes from hearing, and hearing through the word of Christ."

The Word of God will inform our hearts and minds about the will and purpose of God.

Results of Faith
MAKES US AWARE OF AND SECURES FOR US ETERNAL LIFE

John 3:16 "For God so loved the world that He gave his one and only Son, that whosoever believes in him shall not perish but have eternal life."

Connecting Convert

ALLOWS US TO BE MADE INNOCENT, GIVES US PEACE WITH GOD, AND ACCESS TO GOD

Romans 5:1 "Since we have been made right with God by our faith, we have peace with God. This happened through our Lord Jesus Christ, 5:2 who through our faith has brought us into that blessing of God's grace that we now enjoy. And we are happy because of the hope we have of sharing God's glory." ☐

BRINGS SALVATION

Ephesians 2:8 "I mean that you have been saved by grace through believing. You did not save yourselves; it was a gift from God. 5:9 It was not the result of your own efforts, so you cannot brag about it. 5:10 God has made us what we are.

In Christ Jesus, God made us to do good works, which God planned in advance for us to live our lives doing."

As our faith (biblical information) grows and multiplies we are made more knowledgeable in the ways and things of God and, therefore, we are more powerful over the influences of the world. The devil cannot defeat us while we live in harmony with the knowledge we have received.

Experiencing the Word

Is believing in divine truth only, sufficient for salvation? Please read the following passage and formulate your response.

Please read James 2:14-26

What is the essence of the above passage?

_____
_____
_____
_____
_____

_____

What is the above passage indicating about our efforts?

Gordon S. Jones

_____
_____
_____
_____
_____

******DISCIPLER'S TOOL KIT*******

DISCIPLE'S AFFIRMATION AND RESPONSE.
I affirm my faith in Christ and commit to His Word.
Are you willing to claim believing faith?

FROM THIS STUDY THE DISCIPLE(S) SHOULD BE ABLE TO:
1. Define biblical faith.
2. Understand that biblical faith is information.
3. Commit to obeying all that God commands when it is revealed.

REPENTANCE

Repentance is a process that ends in the restoration of one's relationship and fellowship with God and his fellow man. This happens when we receive the Holy Spirit and our minds are transformed and produce new thoughts.

Genuine repentance is a change:

- About sin
- About self
- In attitude and mind
- In actions

The Call to Repentance

The call to repentance permeates the Christian history. This call may be extended in different ways, but the source is always the same.

GOD

Acts 17:30 "In the past God overlooked such ignorance, but now he commands all people everywhere to repent."

The call is a call for an immediate response.

Gordon S. Jones

THE LORD

2 Peter 3:9 "The Lord is not slow in keeping his promise, as some understand slowness. He is patient with you, not wanting anyone to perish, but everyone to come to repentance."

The call is an imperative call to obedience.

PREACHING

Luke 24:47 "and repentance and forgiveness of sins will be preached in his name to all nations, beginning at Jerusalem."

The call is a call to accountability.

We must be very careful that we don't resist or reject God's call to repentance. Rejecting or resisting will grieve the Holy Spirit and grieving the Holy Spirit will deny us eternal life.

The Big Idea
Restoration is not achieved in a single moment. Imagine you are in Austin, Texas and you need to go to Dallas (North). However, you started going south towards San Antonio. You soon discover that you are heading in the wrong direction. There are a few steps needed for heading in the right direction. First, you must admit you are heading in the wrong direction. Second, you must stop going in the wrong direction. Third, you must turn around. Fourth, you must start the process of heading in the right direction. Fifth you must never stop until you eventually reach your destination.

The Result of Repentance

The ultimate result of repentance is the unspeakable joy it brings God. However, there are also bountiful blessings we derive from experiencing genuine repentance.

REPENTANCE RESULTS IN SALVATION FROM SIN'S PENALTY, POWER, AND PRESENCE

2 Corinthians 7:10 "Godly sorrow brings repentance that leads to salvation and leaves no regret, but worldly sorrow brings death."

Notice there is a distinguishable difference between Godly sorrow and worldly sorrow. Theologians have defined them as contrition and attrition respectively. Contrition derives from a contrite heart and attrition is derived from fear of consequences.

REPENTANCE PROVIDES THE CONDITION FOR FORGIVENESS AND THE RECEPTION OF THE HOLY SPIRIT

Acts 2:38 Peter replied, "Repent and be baptized, every one of you, in the name of Jesus Christ for the forgiveness of your sins, and you will receive the gift of the Holy Spirit." (NCV)

REPENTANCE CREATES THE ENVIRONMENT FOR ABUNDANT LIFE

Ezekiel 18:21-23 "But if a wicked man turns away from all the sins he has committed and keeps all my decrees and does what is just and right, he will surely live; he will not die. 22 None of the offenses he has committed will be remembered against him. Because of the righteous things he has done, he will live. 23 Do I take any pleasure in the death of the wicked? Declares the Sovereign LORD. Rather, am I not pleased when they turn from their ways and live?

Please note that an abundant life is not synonymous with a prosperous life.

REPENTANCE EXPUNGES OUR RECORDS OF SINS

Acts 3:19 "Repent, then, and turn to God, so that your sins may be wiped out, that times of refreshing may come from the Lord."

The blotting out (wiping out) of our sinful past is absolutely necessary for us to be in a harmonious relationship with God.

Experiencing the Word

The story of the prodigal son illustrates all the principles of repentance.

Please read Luke 15:

These principles are:

- Acknowledging error (18)
- Being sorry for behavior (19)
- Turning (18, 20)
- Confessing (21)

*******DISCIPLER'S TOOL KIT*******

DISCIPLE'S AFFIRMATION AND RESPONSE

I am out of relationship with Christ and need to experience a change.

Have you truly repented?

FROM THIS STUDY THE DISCIPLE(S) SHOULD BE ABLE TO:

1. State what true repentance is.
2. Understand that repentance is a process.
3. Recognize his/her need for repentance.

CONFESSION

Without confession one will experience irresistible anguish. Confession results in ultimate peace, and where there is peace with God and among Christians, relationships flourish.

Confession is not:

- Providing God with information.
- Speculating.
- Pleading and begging.

Confession is:

- A change in mental attitude, which resulted from repentance.

1 John 1:9 "If we confess our sins, He is faithful and just and will forgive us our sins and purify us from all unrighteousness."

- Acknowledgement of guilt

Proverbs 28:13 "He who conceals his sins does not prosper, but whoever confesses and renounces them finds mercy."

- Asking for forgiveness

Psalm 51:1 "Have mercy on me, O God, according to your unfailing love; according to your great compassion blot out my transgressions."

The Big Idea
Imagine we are standing in a crowded room and I happen to be standing on your toes. You politely expressed to me your discomfort.

There are basically three responses.
1. Ignore you and pretended as if things are okay.
2. Declare I am sorry, but keep standing on your toes.
3. Immediately sympathize with you and remove my foot from your toes.

True confession is the latter.

The legacy of Christ is a twofold peace. It is a peace of friendship and a peace of sweet enjoyment. Spiritual Peace February 19, 1860 by C. H. SPURGEON (1834-1892)

The Power of Confession

READ Psalm 51 and identify the results and power confession brings. For example:

- Confession brings cleansing. (Vs. 7)
- Confession produces rejoicing. (Vs. 12)
- Confession reestablishes and strengthens communion with God. (Vs. 11)
- Confession brings serenity of conscience. (Vs. 13)
- Confession enables a genuine worship experience. (Vs. 14-15)

Connecting Convert

The Recipients of our Confession

The spiritual effects of confession are reconciliation with:

GOD

Hebrews 4:13 "Nothing in all creation is hidden from God's sight. Everything is uncovered and laid bare before the eyes of him to whom we must give account.

THOSE AFFECTED BY OUR ACTIONS

Numbers 5:6-7 Say to the Israelites: 'When a man or woman wrongs another in any way and so is unfaithful to the LORD, that person is guilty and must confess the sin he has committed. He must make full restitution for his wrong, add one fifth to it and give it all to the person he has wronged.

Confession will restore dignity and bring blessings to the life of the believer.

Experiencing the Word

Please READ the following passages and respond to the questions below.

Psalm 32:1

"Blessed is he whose transgressions are forgiven, whose sins are covered."

Psalm 34:18

"The Lord is close to the brokenhearted and saves those who are crushed in spirit."

What is the condition of one who confesses his or her sins and whose sins are forgiven?

_____

_____
_____

_____
_____
_____

Confession brings forgiveness and cleansing. Are you ready to seek forgiveness and experience cleansing?

_____
_____
_____

******DISCIPLER'S TOOL KIT******

DISCIPLE'S AFFIRMATION AND RESPONSE

I acknowledge that my sins are grievous, my faults are many and I need forgiveness.

Are you truly at peace with God and others?

FROM THIS STUDY THE DISCIPLE(S) SHOULD BE ABLE TO:

1. Explain what confession is.
2. Understand that true confession brings peace.
3. Experience forgiveness.

FOR MORE EXPLORATION:

Isaiah 55:7

Micah 7:18

CONVERSION

Conversion from a Christian point of view, conversion means to turn, or change, from the world's way, that is, our own way, to God's Way. (Truly change, not merely as a state of mind, but as a way of life.) This is impossible without the Holy Spirit.

Two aspects of Conversion:

- Birth

Matthew 18:3 "And said, Verily I say unto you, except ye be converted, and become as little children, ye shall not enter into the kingdom of heaven."

John 3:3-5 "Jesus answered and said unto him, verily, verily, I say unto thee, except a man be born again, he cannot see the kingdom of God. Nicodemus saith unto him, how can a man be born when he is old? Can he enter the second time into his mother's womb, and be born? Jesus answered, verily, verily, I say unto thee, except a man be born of water and of the Spirit, he cannot enter into the kingdom of God."

[KEY] There must be a Water and Spirit baptism.

- Growth

2 Peter 3:18 "But grow in grace, and in the knowledge of our Lord and Saviour Jesus Christ. To him be glory both now and for ever. Amen."

Stages of Conversion
- Repentance (recognition and regret)
- Regeneration (a new start)
- Sanctification (getting closer and closer to the goal)
- Glorification (arriving at the final destination)

How is Conversion Achieved?

BY THE HOLY SPIRIT

John 16:7-11 "Nevertheless I tell you the truth; It is expedient for you that I go away: for if I go not away, the Comforter will not come unto you; but if I depart, I will send him unto you. And when he is come, he will reprove the world of sin, and of righteousness, and of judgment: Of sin, because they believe not on me; Of righteousness, because I go to my Father, and ye see me no more; Of judgment, because the prince of this world is judged."

BY THE WORD

James 1: 18 "Of his own will begat he us with the word of truth, that we should be a kind of first fruits of his creatures."

BY REPENTANCE

Acts 3:19 Repent ye therefore, and be converted, that your sins may be blotted out, when the times of refreshing shall come from the presence of the Lord.

BY FAITH IN THE NAME OF JESUS AND HIS ATONEMENT

Acts 4:12 "Neither is there salvation in any other: for there is none other name under heaven given among men, whereby we must be saved."

Connecting Convert

Hindrances to Conversion
- Self- love
- Half-heartedness
- Procrastination
- Excuses

Experiencing the Word

2 Corinthians 5:17 "Therefore if any man be in Christ, he is a new creature: old things are passed away; behold, all things are become new."

Have you experienced a radical change in your worldview? Briefly explain.

_____
_____
_____
_____
_____

************DISCIPLER'S TOOL KIT************

DISCIPLE'S AFFIRMATION

I have decided to make Jesus the Lord of my life.

Are you willing to following Him all the way to baptism?

FROM THIS STUDY THE DISCIPLE(S) SHOULD BE ABLE TO:
1. Explain what conversion is.
2. Understand that true conversion is not a temporary change but a transformation from one thing to another.
3. Commit to baptism.

BAPTISM

It is active faith in the power of God that ultimately secures salvation. Baptism is a ritual for cleansing and a public demonstration of an inner commitment to a new life under God's leadership.

Implicit in the symbolism of baptism:

- Acknowledging there is no other way but God's in the plan of salvation.
- Accepting that deliverance from one's former life is a result of the power of God.
- Committing to obedience to God's way as will be revealed. Proverbs 4:18.

Biblical Steps for Baptism

Acts 2: 37 – 38 When the people heard this, they were cut to the heart and said to Peter and the other apostles, Brothers, what shall we do?" Peter replied, "Repent and be baptized, every one of you, in the name of Jesus Christ for the forgiveness of your sins. And you will receive the gift of the Holy Spirit."

1. Instruction
2. Belief - in the provision of salvation in Jesus.

3. Repentance- turn from sin
4. Conversion- return to God

Biblical method and formula for baptism

METHOD (Immersion)

John 3:23 "And John also was baptizing in Aenon near to Salim, because there was much water there: and they came, and were baptized."

FORMULA (Father, Son, and Holy Spirit)

Matthew 28:18-20 "Then Jesus came to them and said, "All authority in heaven and on earth has been given to me. 19Therefore go and make disciples of all nations, baptizing them in the name of the Father and of the Son and of the Holy Spirit, 20and teaching them to obey everything I have commanded you. And surely I am with you always, to the very end of the age."

The Big Idea
When Jesus was baptized three significant things are reported to have happened and these will also happen to each person that is baptized.

Matthew 3: 13 -17

- Acceptance in heaven (Heaven was opened)
- Acquisition of Holy Spirit (dove lighted on His head)
- Acquittal from sins (Voice from Heaven proclaimed, "This is My Beloved Son.")

Experiencing the Word

Romans 6: 1- 11 "What shall we say, then? Shall we go on sinning so that grace may increase? 2By no means! We died to sin; how can we live in it any longer? 3Or don't you know that all of us who were baptized into Christ Jesus were baptized into his death? 4We were therefore buried with him through baptism into death in order that, just as Christ was raised from the dead through the glory of the Father, we too may live a new life. 5If we have been united with him like this in his death, we will certainly also be united with him in his resurrection. 6For we know that our old self was crucified with him so that

the body of sin might be done away with, that we should no longer be slaves to sin—"

7 because anyone who has died has been freed from sin. 8Now if we died with Christ, we believe that we will also live with him. 9For we know that since Christ was raised from the dead, he cannot die again; death no longer has mastery over him. 10The death he died, he died to sin once for all; but the life he lives, he lives to God. 11In the same way, count yourselves dead to sin but alive to God in Christ Jesus."

Baptism signifies:

- Death
- Burial
- Resurrection

******DISCIPLER'S TOOL KIT******

DISCIPLE'S AFFIRMATION AND RESPONSE

I have decided to become a member of the body of Christ pending baptism.

Note: Have candidate fill out Baptismal Questionnaire. (page 29).

ASK CANDIDATE TO COMMIT TO:

- Personal daily devotion.
- Attending church services.

Connecting Convert

- Discipleship classes for one month.

REMEMBER TO:

Set up an appointment with Pastor and candidate for the final baptismal preparation.

NOTES TO PASTOR/ PASTORAL DESIGNEE

Objectives:

- Congratulate candidate on the decision to become a disciple of Christ and a member of the body of Christ
- Arrange arrival time at church prior to baptism.

Describe baptismal process, and where necessary have demonstration

REMEMBER TO INFORM CANDIDATE:

To bring a complete change of clothes to wear in the water.

That towels are provided by deaconesses.

That bathing caps or shower caps are optional.

Sample
Baptismal Questionnaire
(Please Print)
Name: _____

Address: _____

City: _____ State: _____

Phone: ( ) _____ Email: _____

Date of Birth: _____

Please list family members
_____
_____
_____

Favorite Bible Text(s)
_____
_____
_____

I desire to become a member of the _____ Church pending baptism.

Signature_____

Date: _____

*********DISCIPLER'S TOOL KIT**********

Demographics of Class

The disciples or class may be constituted of the following sources

Connecting Convert

- Newly baptized members
- New profession of faith members
- Prospective members

Processing Prospective Members
- Collect full name and contact information for each student.
- Celebrate the decision for membership
- Communicate the steps in the process towards mature membership.
- Schedule time and place for continued studies.

Successfully Relating to Prospective Members' Demands
- Being polite
- Being prayerful
- Being prepared
- Being punctual

Goals:
- Provide spiritual, mental, and emotional education to the student.
- Train the student on how to be a disciple for Jesus Christ.
- Provide encouragement and caring contact for the student.

Objective:
Use the Bible & doctrinal materials in assisting the student to develop a positive relationship with Jesus Christ and the church.

- Use the provided tools to identify the student's spiritual gifts and assist him/her in ministry placement.

- Empower and equip students to become disciples and disciplers.

CONNECTING TO THE PURPOSE OF CHRIST

Essentials for Christian Growth

A Practical Guide to Understanding the Basic process toward Christian Maturity

"But grow in grace, and in the knowledge of our Lord and Savior Jesus Christ. To him be glory both now and for ever. Amen."
2 Peter 3: 18

Gordon S. Jones

EVERYONE HAS TO OBEY

"The great principles of God's Law are embodied in the Ten Commandments found in Exodus and exemplified in the life of Christ. They express God's love, God's will and God's purposes concerning human conduct and relationships, and are binding upon all people in every age. These precepts are the basis of God's covenant with His people and the standard of God's judgment." (Matt. 22: 36 - 40)

The commandments in Exodus 20: 3– 11 expresses both principle and precept.

A precept is a specific rule, prescribing a certain action under certain circumstances. A principle is a general guideline, intended to result in different actions under a variety of circumstances.

1. The first commandment demonstrates the principle of loyalty.

2. The second commandment demonstrates the principle of worship

3. The third commandment demonstrates the principle of reverence.

4. The fourth commandment demonstrates the principle of sanctification.

5. The fifth commandment demonstrates the principle of respect for authority.
6. The sixth commandment demonstrates the principle of respect for life.
7. The seventh commandment demonstrates the principle of purity.
8. The eighth commandment demonstrates the principle of honesty.
9. The ninth commandment demonstrates the principle of truthfulness.
10. The tenth commandment demonstrates the principle of contentment.

Note we are saved by faith and faith alone but genuine "faith must reach a point where it will control the affections and impulses of the heart."

God's Holy Sabbath

After six days of creation, God instituted the Sabbath as a memorial of His creative work. The fourth commandment requires observance of the seventh day Sabbath. Jesus and the apostles observed this day, teaching that it is a memorial of creation and redemption and a special time for worship and communion with God. (Ex. 20: 8 - 11)

Three distinct acts by which God created the Sabbath (Gen. 2: 1-3)-

- Blessed it
- Sanctified it
- Rested on it

How to celebrate the Sabbath-

- Evening to evening (Lev. 23: 32)
- Principle (Isaiah 58: 13, 14)

God's Stewardship Laws

We are God's stewards, entrusted by Him with resources of time, talents, treasure and temple. We must acknowledge God's ownership by faithfully worshipping Him, by sacrificially service to our fellow men, and by loyally supporting the proclamation of His gospel and the support and growth of His church.

Stewards
- Recognize God's ownership. (Psalms 50: 10 – 12)
- Are totally committed in every area of their lives. (1 Cor. 10: 31)
- Are blessed by their faithfulness. (Malachi 3: 10 - 12)

God's Standards on Christian Behavior

As we compare the moral and ethical decline in society with the manner of life that God approves, we are more conscious of our responsibility to practice and teach Christ's standards for Christian behavior. God has a right to desire a love that will be demonstrated in trust and obedience.

What are God's great claims on us? (1 Cor. 6: 19, 20)
- Created us
- Redeemed us

There are more than one thousand texts in Scripture that deal with God's standards on health, adornment, and entertainment.

God's Standards on Health

- Original (Genesis 1: 29)
- First modification (Genesis 3: 18)
- Second modification (Genesis 6: 1 Gen 7: 14; Gen 9: 3; Lev. 11: 1 - 20)
- Additions (Prov. 20:1)

God's Standards on Adornment
- Modesty (1 Tim. 2: 9, 10)
- Not outward (1 Pet. 3: 3 - 5)

God's Standards on Entertainment
- Glorify God in everything (1 Cor. 10: 31)
- Guard the avenues to the mind (Matt. 15: 18 - 20)

******DISCIPLER'S TOOL KIT******

Objectives:
- Identify the great principles in God's Law.
- Explain the importance of:
    - Observing God's Holy Sabbath.
    - God's stewardship Laws.
    - God's standards on health.
    - God's standards on adornment.
    - God's standards on entertainment.
    - God's standards on Christian behavior.

PREPARING FOR THIS CLASS YOU WILL NEED:
- Have daily devotional book for each disciple to encourage daily study
- Church bulletins for each student to encourage attendance to church services

Gordon S. Jones

EVERYONE HAS TO SUBMIT

Biblical submission is more than surrendering to those in authority over us. It is a mutual voluntary act of allegiance, support, and responsibility for each other.

The family institution is the first demonstration of submission and was divinely established in the Garden of Eden and affirmed by Jesus. A happy, healthy, well-functioning family provides and fosters a climate conducive to a better relationship with the Lord and a stronger witness to the community around us.

- God's picture of the family (Eph. 5:21-33)
- Permanency of the family (Matt. 5:31,32)

The Christian church is the second demonstration of submission and represents the community of believers who accept Jesus Christ as Savior and Lord. As Head of the church, Christ leads us in worship, fellowship and service.

Five metaphors help define what the church is:

1. John 10: 2 - 5, 11 - Shepherd of the sheep.
2. 1 Cor. 12: 27 - ye are the body of Christ.
3. Eph. 2: 19 - fellow citizens with the saints, and of the household of God.

Connecting Convert

4. 1 Pet. 2: 5 - ye also, as living stones, are built up a spiritual house, an holy priesthood.
5. Rev. 19: 7 - 8 - for the marriage of the Lamb is come, and His wife has made herself ready.

Two other structures of submission are expected of every child of God:

Government, and our Employers

- Romans 13: 1 submission to government authority
- Colossians 3: 22, 4:1 submission to our employers.

******DISCIPLER'S TOOL KIT******

Objectives:

- Emphasize the concept of biblical submission.
- Explain the importance of the polity.
- Introduce the forms of church governance.
- Discuss the constituent levels of your church

PREPARING FOR THIS CLASS YOU WILL NEED:

- To plan class breakfast or an occasion to introduce the new disciple to other disciples.
- To invite Church Board members.
- Have copies of important Church documents for each new disciple.

REMEMBER TO:

Plan class breakfast to introduce new disciples to church officers. It's expected that key church officers be invited to meet with the class or disciple.

Gordon S. Jones

EVERYONE HAS TO PARTICIPATE

Spiritual gifts are special abilities given by the Holy Spirit and distributed to every believer according to God's design and grace for the body of Christ.

The Bible presents five clear truths about the spiritual gifts.

1. First, every Christian has at least one gift (I Cor. 12:7; Rom. 12:6-8; I Pet. 4:10).
2. God gives the church all the gifts it needs to be His people and do His will (I Cor. 12:11, 18).
3. Using a spiritual gift builds up both God's Kingdom and the believer (I Cor. 12:7; I Cor. 14:12).
4. God expects every Christian to discover, develop, and use his gift(s) (I Cor. 12:1).
5. Spiritual gifts must operate with the Fruit of the Spirit (Gal. 5:22-23).

Romans 12:6-8	**1 Corinthians 12**
Exhortation	Wisdom
Giving	Knowledge
Leadership	Faith
Mercy	Healing

Connecting Convert

Prophecy	Miracles
Service	Prophecy
Teaching	Discernment of Spirit
	Kinds of Tongues
	Interpretation of Tongues
1 Peter 4: 9	**1 Timothy 2**
Craftsmanship	Hospitality
Exodus 31: 3 – 5	**Psalm 150: 3 - 5**
Craftsmanship	Creativity
	Communications

**********DISCIPLER'S TOOL KIT**********

Objectives:

- Outline steps toward participating in Ministry -
- Study the Scriptures
- Identify giftedness
- Match the gift with the ministry

Emphasize the key purpose for giftedness (service) -

- Inward (nurturing each other)
- Outward (evangelism)

PREPARING FOR THIS CLASS YOU WILL NEED:

- To contact the ministry placement team or those responsible for assignment new disciples to ministries in your church

- To have copies of the Spiritual Gifts Inventory for each new disciple of the class.

After biblically leading disciple(s) in identifying spiritual gifts, lead disciple(s) in taking Spiritual Gift Inventory and discuss possible ministry involvement.

EVERYONE HAS TO WITNESS

The greatest need in the body of Christ is not better programs, methods or tools, but better equipped men and women who know their Redeemer personally, men and women who catch His vision and feel His passion for the world, men and women who are willing to sacrifice everything that the mission might be everything.

Acts 1: 8

When the Spirit is received we become witnesses for Christ.

Please read Matthew 28:18 -20 (this expresses our corporate purpose)

Notice:

The mandate in verse 19

What directly precedes it in verse 18 (divine authority and power)

What directly follows it in verse 20 (divine promise of His everlasting presence)

We are conditioned to fear failure. As a result we do not attempt certain things simply because we fear that we might fail. Imagine all the great things you could have achieved if only you had simply tried.

There are three categories of fear that we struggle with when witnessing to others.

1. The fear of inadequacy
2. The fear of rejection
3. The fear of failure

Spiritual remedies (2 Timothy 1:7)

- God's gift of power will banish the fear of inadequacy.
- The gift of love will eliminate the fear of rejection.
- The gift of discipleship removes the fear of failure.

************DISCIPLER'S TOOL KIT************

Objectives:

- Explain the biblical mandate for witnessing.
- Identify six progressive stages to Christ's method of witnessing. Ministry of Healing .p143
    - Socializing with others
    - Desiring the good of others
    - Empathizing with others
    - Ministering to others
    - Winning the confidence of others
- Have each member of class identify and commit to influencing one person for Christ within three months.

PREPARING FOR THIS CLASS YOU WILL NEED:

- To contact Discipleship Minister.
- Prepare to take names of class evangelistic interests.

Connecting Convert

REMEMBER TO:

- Encourage new disciples to submit names of individuals they would like to see becoming disciples.

- Encourage new disciples to start inviting others in a discipleship relationship.

- Ask member if they would be interested in learning how to conduct a bible study.

ABOUT THE AUTHOR

Dr. Gordon is the Ministerial Director and Evangelism Coordinator of the Southwest Region Conference of Seventh-day Adventist. He is also the Senior Pastor of the Alpha Seventh-day Adventist Church in Austin, Texas.

Made in the USA
Columbia, SC
01 November 2024